Now You Know: Work You Can Do

Encyclopaedia Britannica Educational Corporation Chicago/Toronto

Now You Know:
Work You Can Do

Author
Anne Neigoff

Designer
Paul McNear

Artists
Muriel and Jim Collins

Consultants
Mary K. Lawler, Co-ordinator of Elementary Guidance
Chicago Public Schools
Chicago, Illinois

Deborah Partridge Wolfe, Professor of Education
Queens College, City University of New York
Flushing, New York

Encyclopaedia Britannica Educational Corporation

4

Do you ever sit and dream
   about all the wonderful things
   you could be or do?
Maybe you make believe
   that you are in a space rocket,
   zooming to the moon.
Maybe you pretend
   that you are a detective
   or a television star.

It is fun to pretend
   and dream.
But it is even more fun
   to make your dreams
   come true.
Someday you will go to work.
What work would you really like to do?
What would you really like to be?

You can be almost anything you want to be.
You can do many things right now.
What do you like to do?
Do you like to run a race
              or climb a tree?
Maybe you like to whistle. Wheeeee!
It is fun to do things at home,
   and in school,
   and with your friends.
Could you do all these things last year, too?

Every day you can do more things.
You can read and write more words.
You can build a better wagon.
You can go more places all by yourself.
You know how to find out more things
   all by yourself, too!
Do you feel proud as you do more things,
   learn more things,
   grow and grow and grow?

Every day when you are awake,
   and when you are sleeping,
   you are growing taller and stronger.
Every day you can do more things.
When you are at home,
            and in school,
            and with your friends,
   you are learning new things to do.
How do you learn new things?

How did you learn to ride your bicycle?
Do you remember how it wobbled and wobbled
    and then fell over?
But you tried and tried and tried,
    and now you can ride to your friend's home,
                    ride to the store,
                    ride many places!
Sometimes you have to try to do a new thing
    over and over and over again.
Then how proud you are when you can do it!
It is fun to ride a bicycle.
Can you fix your own bicycle, too?
Do you like to fix things?
Would you like to learn how to fix
    bicycles or cars or maybe a space rocket?

9

How many different kinds of things
   do you like to do?
Did you ever write them all down?
Just for fun, try!
Sometimes you like to work alone
   to draw a picture,
     read a book,
10   or make a model sailboat.

Do you ever make believe that the wind
   will blow you and your sailboat
   to places far away?
Would you like to sail and sail
   across the ocean someday
   and write a story about it?

You have to work alone
   when you write a story.
Do you think you would like to work
   alone most of the time?

11

Sometimes you do not want to work alone.
You do not want to talk to your sister
                              or brother
                              or best friend.
Who do you want to talk to? Your dog!
He always understands everything you say.
He always understands how you feel.
You can throw a stick, and he will bring it back.
You can play with him and teach him tricks.
You like to take care of him, too.
Would you like to work with animals?

What kind of work would you like to do?
You could be an animal doctor.
You could take care of animals in a zoo.
Maybe you would like to teach dogs
   how to help people who cannot see.
There are many ways to work with animals.
Which way would you choose?

Sometimes you like to be with other people.
You like to go fishing with your father.
You like to do homework with your sister.
Does she ever help you with your homework?
Do you help her, too?
Sometimes it is fun to work and play
  with your friends.
You can play games and tell secrets.
You can have a fair in your backyard.
What fun it is!

You all have different ideas.
You all want to do different things.
But you all work together
  and have a wonderful time!
What would you like best?
Would you like to work alone?
Would you like to work with other people?   15

Sometimes you want to do two things
at the same time.
Maybe your mother is busy.
You know it will help her
if you take care of your little sister.
You want to help your mother,
but you want to go to the playground
with your friends, too.
What do you do?
How does it make you feel?

Sometimes you take care of your little sister.
You play with her, and she has fun.
Do you have fun, too?
Do you ever teach her new things to do?
Would you like to be a teacher
  and teach boys and girls in school?

Your teacher works in school.
You work in school, too.
You work to learn about numbers.
You use numbers every day
    at home and with your friends, too.
You count, "Strike one, strike two, strike three!"
The batter is out in the baseball game.
Is that work or fun?
How many other ways
    do you use numbers every day?

When you go to work, you will use numbers
    every day, too.
Where will you work?
The place has a number.
What bus will you take?
The bus has a number, too.
How much money will you get?
If you grow things, make things,
    sell things, or do things,
    you will use numbers.
Are you glad you learn about numbers
    in school?

Every day you use numbers
   in different ways.
Sometimes you use them
   to measure things.
How tall are you?
You measure against a wall.
Are you taller than last year?
How much taller are you?
The numbers on a ruler tell you.

When you build something,
   you measure, too.
You make sure each piece of wood
   is just the right size.
Then all the pieces
   will fit together.
Would you like
   to build a house someday?

Did you ever cook something?
You put in some of this.
You put in some of that.
You measure each thing you put in.
Then you mix the things together.
What did you cook?
Did it taste good when it was done?
Would you like to be a cook
  in a restaurant?

When you go to school,
  you learn to read and write, too.
How many different kinds of things
  do you read and write every day?
You read what the teacher writes
  on the chalkboard.
You write your homework,
  and the teacher reads it.
You read a note from your mother.
You write a note, too.
How do the things you read or write
  help you have fun and learn things
  and find out what is happening?

BOX XYZ ... THE NEWS ... GENTLEMEN...
YOUR ADVERTISMENT FOR A BOOKSTORE MANAGER
INTERESTED ME VERY MUCH.   I WOULD LIKE
TO WORK .....

When you go to work,
   you will have to read and write
   many different kinds of things.
Maybe you will write letters to say
   you want to buy things.
Maybe you will write letters to say
   you want to sell things.
You will write to people you cannot see,
   but they can read what you write.
You can read what they write, too.

24

When you write, you can talk to people
    who are far, far away.
Sometimes the people know you.
Sometimes the people do not know you,
    but they can read what you write.
You can write a story or a poem to tell
    what you think or feel or imagine.
You can write an advertisement, too,
    to help people know what to buy
    and where to buy it.
Did you ever try to write an advertisement?
It is fun to try.

Just imagine that you have to sell
    the new kittens your cat had.
How furry and pouncy the kittens are!
You like them, and you want somebody
    to like and want them, too.
What will you write in your advertisement?
How are you helping somebody who wants
    to get a kitten?
Would you like to write advertisements
    to help people buy
    what they need and want?

Sometimes you like to do this.
Sometimes you like to do that.
Sometimes you change your mind
  right in the middle of what you are doing!
What do you do then?
Do you stop playing a game
  because you are losing?
What do your friends say to you?
Are you angry when somebody else stops playing
26   before the game is finished?

When you begin something,
   you are making a promise to finish it.
It is easy to begin playing a game,
         begin drawing a picture for school,
         begin making a dollhouse
   for your little sister.
But sometimes it is hard
   to make yourself finish.
Sometimes you have to work and work.
How happy and proud you are
   when you finish!
Who else is happy?
What would happen if these workers
   did not finish their jobs?

How many people are you?
Just one YOU!
But you do not talk in the same way
   to your mother,
   to your father,
   to your teacher,
   and to your best friend.
You do not do things in the same way
   at home and at school
   and when you play with your friends.

You do not do the same things with all
   of your friends.
Maybe some like to ride horses,
   and some like to ride bicycles.
Some like to do puppet plays,
   and some like to make model planes.
It is fun to do different things
   with each friend.
It is fun to make new friends and try
   new things to do.
Could you do what these workers are doing?
Would you like to try?

What do you like best to do?
Every day you are finding out.
You are trying new things to do,
     learning new things to do,
     doing new things.
Every day you are finding out
   that you can be almost anything
   you want to be!

What would you like to do?
We need many people
   to grow and make, sell and do,
   the things that help us
   live and work and play.

We need people to help us
   keep our land and air and water clean.
Maybe you will help do that.
What would you like to do
   to help people live and grow?

What work are these people doing?
What work would you like to do?